Cars

by Mike Patrick

HOUGHTON MIFFLIN   BOSTON • MORRIS PLAINS, NJ

California • Colorado • Georgia • Illinois • New Jersey • Texas

I like this red car.
It is a new car.

I like this black car.
It is an old car.

I like this red car.
It is a small car.

I like this white car.
It is a long car.

I like this blue car.
It is a fast car.

I like this yellow car.
It is a toy car.

But I like these cars
the best.